# Scott Free

## TINA GRIMES

# It Smells Like Smoke and Mirrors

As the stale smell of Benson and Hedges danced on a slight Texas breeze, I sat on the back porch of our home in a metal patio chair facing my mother. Anytime I was singled out, I immediately went into defense mode. *What did I do now? Why am I being called out here alone?* I waited while she smoked her cigarette.

"I need to know what you remember from your childhood."

Confused, I looked up, quickly meeting her gaze. The moment she took another drag from her cigarette, I understood what she was fishing for. My childhood was mostly random puzzle pieces I couldn't make fit. There were a few, however, that instantly made the hairs on the back of my neck stand up. Unable to give a straight answer when put on the spot, I deflected.

"What do you mean?"

With a deep exhale and a cloud of smoke, she went full speed ahead. I abhorred her disgusting habit. When she would get mad at me for God knows what, she would blow it directly in my face. Enduring cigarette smoke in my face was one thing, but the fact that she knew I was allergic to it was a completely different concept.

"When you were little, you went to a home daycare, and something happened to you. I want to know if you remember any of it."

She took a few more drags, crossed her thin right leg over her left and started nervously bouncing. She reminded me of Big Bird with black stirrup pants on. The oversized tee shirt made her appear top heavy, while the stirrup pants that clung to her long skinny legs made her appear anorexic. Her hair was disheveled, having slept most of the day after three straight night shifts at the hospital. I often wondered how a nurse could sit there and smoke cigarettes, knowing the repercussions that would catch up with her later in life. My mind began racing as I sat there staring at the ground and fidgeting with my hands. It played a horrible movie of buried secrets I wish I never owned or starred in for that matter. Flashes of images containing my tiny body being pushed against walls, pinched and thumped by caregivers, and a large man meeting my naked body on the floor permeated my mind.

"There was a home daycare near our neighborhood that you attended for a while. A man everyone called Papa Joe owned and ran it."

As she tapped the burning end of her pleasure stick on the concrete ground, I very vividly had a flash of a ghost walking around our porch.

"Did he wear red shirts all the time and black pants?"

As she nodded her head, I continued asking questions while the ghost of a man I knew but couldn't remember walked past me and disappeared.

"Did he wear glasses? Was he older?"

At this point, I did not know who I was seeing or what my mind was unveiling. I calmly sat there and allowed myself to recall forgotten memories. Was this what a flashback was? Was this real-life right now? Curious, I wanted to know why this conversation was happening, right at that moment, right at that point in time. Before now, nobody had ever taken the time to find out what happened to me. Hyper focused, emotions came flooding through like a massive dam bursting open. Scared, sad, anxious, curious, ignorant, dirty, shameful, gut-wrenching feelings overcame me. Grasping the arms of the chair, I catapulted myself back to reality.

"Mom, why are you asking me this now? Why is this important today?"

Lighting another cigarette between her bony fingers and pursing her dry lips around it, she exhaled louder.

"I do not know exactly what he did to you, but I know when I picked you up on your third birthday, you came out of the bathroom with one shoe on and one shoe off. Your clothes were disheveled. I knew something was wrong."

My right leg began bouncing and shaking uncontrollably and I bit my bottom lip. Anxiety, worry, fear, shame, guilt, and absolute nakedness overwhelmed me.

"He forced my clothes back on and threw my shoes at me."

The words just flew out of my mouth with little to no effort. I could not stop them. I could not erase them like I could if I wrote them on paper. There was no way to box them

3

back up or shove them to the back of the dusty shelf they had resided on for the last ten years. My thoughts were all over the place as I tried to make sense of my crumbling world. Any foundation I thought I had disappeared. She pushed and kept going, despite any obvious signs of discomfort. Even if I wanted to avoid, deflect, and run, I couldn't. I felt trapped by my own mother. I felt sudden feelings of betrayal, abandonment, and most importantly, being unlovable.

"You were such a scared little child. Your persistent speech problems kept all of us in the dark. Do you remember your speech therapist? She worked so hard with you. You couldn't even say 'mama'."

My heart warmed at the thought of her. Even when my mother dropped me off crying, my therapist scooped me up and just held me. She was always so gentle and kind. Reflecting on my time with her, I knew she was a safe harbor in the stormy seas of my life. The cherished thoughts of her instantly calmed me. She did not just teach me how to talk. She taught me how to trust. How to keep loving others. Her fierce love of God protected my heart, and it wouldn't be until much later that I would fully understand just how much so.

"I will never forget her. I miss her. Her hugs always soothed me."

For the first time since she started this conversation, I smiled. She let out another cloud of smoke before barreling forward.

"Papa Joe died a few days ago."

Was this somehow supposed to create feelings of relief and happiness? If so, why wasn't I feeling that now? On a day that started out just as ordinary as any other summer day, I now found myself feeling like a scared three-year-old trying to shove her shoes on without crying so nobody would know my secret.

"I have struggled with my memories. I am missing pieces of my childhood. Why are you just now trying to understand what happened to me? Why now?"

Anger overcame my senses. I didn't understand why my ability to recollect things was so fragmented and fractured. Blurry puzzle pieces of lost memories were fitting together and becoming clear. As they were starting to make sense, I quickly wondered why professional help such as counseling had not been an option growing up. While I still had many holes in my memory, one thing was certain. From an incredibly early age, I was utterly and completely traumatized and could do nothing about it. Or so I thought.

"I pulled you out of that daycare and never took you back. He was a very dangerous man."

While she continued fidgeting with her cigarette, I looked directly at her with curiosity.

"Did you report it?"

She exhaled in annoyance. The uneasy feeling of being a burden to her came creeping back in.

"Yes, I did everything a good mother should do. I reported it but you wouldn't speak. You were so scared. You wouldn't even let your baby sister speak about it. He walked away free because you wouldn't tell anyone what he did to you."

She put her cigarette out and quietly ended the conversation. I was reeling from everything we just spoke about. I had so many questions, but nobody could answer them except me. Sadly, I couldn't even answer them because my mind blocked the most horrific parts of what happened. I didn't know it at that moment, but my mother's last statement putting the blame of his freedom on my shoulders would haunt me for years to come.

# Objects in Mirrors are as False as They Appear

Summers in Texas can be brutal, but it never stopped my baby sister and me from playing outside. The majority of our childhood was enjoyed outdoors. We would roller-blade, ride bikes, walk, and even adventure into the woods surrounding our new home. When we lived at the new house with our mother, stepfather, and older sister, my baby sister and I spent most of our time exploring the surrounding woods. We discovered areas unknown to us. Our imaginations ran rampant and so did we. Around the trees, up the hills, down the hills, through the creek, and back again. The woods didn't scare me. I wandered all around the acre of land we lived on. I was carefree, content, and even overjoyed here. My baby sister and I were always together. We were only nineteen months apart. Our summer days slipped through our fingertips without us realizing. Our façade of happiness there didn't last.

I still remember my mother divorcing my dad some ten years before. Their years together were riddled with arguing, hitting, yelling, and kicking. The tension between both households was palpable. My dad was angry at my mother, but my mother was downright vicious about my dad. Every chance she got, she made sure to tell me how he always said I wasn't his. Hearing this so often, I believed it. I fully believed he merely tolerated me rather than truly loved me. It was hard living full time with someone always willing to tell me how she was the only parent who truly loved me and then be subjected to going to my dad's every other weekend to wonder if he did everything for me out of love or out of some saintly duty just because I bore his last name. Nonetheless, this was my life at that point.

Unfortunately, my mother found herself struggling to make ends meet with three children under the age of ten when they divorced. An empty fridge, bare cabinets, swarms of flying bugs plagued us. There was no silver lining to be found. My ten-year-old sister should not have had to tend to two toddlers while their struggling mother was working and going to school. Yet, she did. She smiled and played with us despite the horrid circumstances our mother and father thrust us in. When food was absent, love and homemade ice tray pops to avoid starvation were aplenty. My sister made sure of it.

One night during this time, my mother came home after work with a friend. I had never seen her before. They talked and laughed while we remained invisible. Invisible was easy. Invisible was the way she preferred us; therefore, we liked it too. If we stayed invisible, we didn't get yelled at as often.

"This is my friend. She is in beauty school."

My mother was in a good mood for a change. I smiled but kept quiet. Much later, I noticed she had a towel on her head. Curiosity got the better of me. I wanted, no, I needed to know what was going on underneath that towel on my mother's head. Her friend started towel-drying her hair. Was it happening soon? I could not sit still with all the anticipation building up inside me. Alas, the towel came off and I was speechless. Not a good speechless.

Have you ever seen pink that was so pastel, it was almost purple? Have you ever seen the color of a unicorn's mane and tail? How about a mermaid tail? It was not quite like any of those. She looked like a fish out of water. Literally. Hair in a pink shade of salmon slowly fell out of the towel and hung limp around her face. Whatever friendship they had before was sure to end. Before I knew it, they were both gone and it was quiet. I did not see my mother again until the next morning. Her hair was brown again. Thank God. I could not take her out looking like a LaLa Loopsy doll on crack.

Our days together as a family of four ended abruptly. My older sister Lyn moved in with my dad while my baby sister and I moved in with our Nannie. Nannie was the sweetest woman I ever knew. She was my mother's mom. She was loving, funny, silly, warm, and kind. Never a cuss word out of her mouth. She made sure we went to church every Sunday. As our mother rode off into the sunset leaving us in her rearview, I still felt betrayed and abandoned. How could someone drive off while watching their children fall apart in the rearview mirror? Part of me felt dirty, shameful, bad, guilty, and unlovable again. I cried off and on for days. All I wanted was to be held by my mother despite the unstable relationships she had with others. Nannie filled my days with laughter, hugs, love, food, and stability. Sadly, that wouldn't last forever either. Nothing ever did.

My dad remarried a few years after my mother started college. She brought about a new sense of stability. My weekends spent at his house were filled with fishing, shooting BB guns, and digging bones out of the ground. We often spent time out at the farm where my Mammaw and Pappaw lived. I enjoyed visiting my dad's parents. His mom always made the best homemade biscuits and cobblers. Sometimes, we would pick the fruit for the cobblers from the backyard for Mammaw. Spending time there was peaceful, but I still had that nagging thought in my mind that my daddy didn't love me and didn't believe I was his biological daughter. I felt like an outcast everywhere I went. My baby sister seemed to be his favorite. She was the most like him. My dad loved hunting. I did not. He also loved deer meat. I abhorred it. My baby sister loved it all. I was jealous of my baby sister at times because it always seemed she did no wrong in my dad's eyes. I on the other hand was always in trouble with him. I guess I couldn't do anything right anywhere I went.

My dad's parents lived on farmland that had been in my Mammaw's family for over a hundred years. The red dirt lane that led to their home was part of the original El Camino Real too. It was rich in history from the Scott family lineage. My mother's voice kept echoing in my mind.

*Your dad doesn't even believe you are his, but he said he would still love you since you had his last name. I never cheated on your dad, but he sure believed I did.*

From an early age, I felt unlovable. My mother didn't love us enough to stay and my daddy didn't love me for me. I believed he just loved me because I had his last name.

For more than half my life, I believed every ounce of me was Scott-free. I believed every lie my mother ever told me regarding my dad's love or lack of love for me. I didn't want to be Scott-free, but here I was, torn between truth and lies. Torn between a vengeful mother and a hurting father.

I often thought back to those times while playing with my sister in the woods at our new house. We had come a long way from the run-down trailer park in the seedy neighborhood on the south side of town with bare cabinets and homemade ice pops. Living with Nannie was the best thing that ever happened to us. She was a wonderful caregiver and grandmother. My dad ended up divorced again a few years after he remarried. Nine months after having a son, my stepmom and my brother moved out of town to her hometown of Plano. I felt abandoned again. I was almost ready to call her mom. She had been a wonderful mother figure for me for the short time they were married.

When my mother returned seven years later, with her nursing degree behind her, she had a new man in her life. She arrived to rip us from the main source of stability we ever had. We fought. We cried. We begged. Seven years with random contact few and far between, but here she was. Ready to take possession of her recycled property yet again.

"You are such a crybaby. Always so emotional. You knew Nannie wasn't permanent. I was always coming back. I had to go to school to make a better life for us. Say your goodbyes and let's go."

Touching. Abandon your children for seven years under the guise of making a better life. No choice was given to us. My Nannie's hands were tied. I did not want this. My Nannie did not want this. I didn't agree to be passed around like a rag doll. Change was hard. I despised it, but off I went.

It quickly became clear to me that my mother had pulled us from Nannie's once she was set to remarry. Her new husband's ready-made family ended his bachelor days. His willing partnership ended her struggles as a single mother. It was a win-win for both of them. Within the first year of their marriage, their custom-built home was complete. The house was amazing. My baby sister and I shared a room. Our older sister had her own room. For the first time in our lives, we had a real home with an acre of woods. The same woods we loved frolicking through.

Nannie's house had been the only home we knew for the majority of our lives. Our new home gave the illusion of hope, stability, and togetherness. When you walked in the front door, you had the living room to the left. I had never seen cathedral ceilings in a home until now. Beautiful windows allowed the gorgeous natural light to flow through the living room and across the built-in shelves. To the right of the entryway, there were three doors.

The first door was my baby sister's and my bedroom. It was bigger than any room we had shared prior to this. Our closet was a walk-in closet with shelving. The second door was a bathroom that had one entrance from the hallway and one from my older sister's room. Her room was the third door. She also had a walk-in closet.

Down the hardwood-lined hallway, there were two directions you could go. Left to the kitchen, or right to my stepdad's and my mother's bedroom. The bedroom was enormous. It had a huge walk-in closet with shelving and a massive bathroom. French doors led to the bathroom that housed a jetted tub, double sink, toilet, and shower. Their room even had French doors going to the outdoor patio where my mother decided to figure out things about my childhood she should have tended to years before.

The kitchen was amazing. Countertops made the usual outline of the kitchen, but a catty-cornered island of counter-tops held the double sink in the middle of the room. There was a nice breakfast nook and a formal dining room just off the kitchen. It all looped back around to the living room. The new house was good, but like all good things, this too ended just as quickly as it started.

# I Am My Sister's Keeper

After our talk on the patio, my mother and I both went back inside the house. I went to my room.

"What did she want, sissy?"

I plopped down on my daybed against the wall facing my baby sister. Between our two matching daybeds, there was one huge window with an arch. A custom-made shade covered the massive glass. The soft pink perfectly coordinated with our J.C. Penney catalog floral bedding. I stared up at the window as the sunlight filtered through.

"Well, she wanted to know if I remembered something from my childhood. Something about a man everyone called Papa Joe."

With that, she hopped off her matching bed and climbed into mine. I stared at my feet dangling from the edge of my bed and felt her little arm wrap around my shoulders.

"Really? Who was he?"

A flash of memory instantly came forward. A memory of my baby sister dancing and singing.

"Papa Joe broke my wee-wee. Papa Joe broke my wee-wee."

I refused to be the reason my baby sister dredged up any horrific memories. I shrugged and hugged her tight.

"Let's go explore the woods again!"

Her face brightened up and off we went. Up the hills, down the hills, around the trees, and through the creek. My baby sister and I didn't always get along, but that day, I made sure we did. I would not be the reason her day went downhill like mine.

My mother did not mention Papa Joe again, and I didn't dare mention him to her either. I could not believe how stupid I was for not telling anyone he molested me. Where was my justice? Where were the other kids' justice from the daycare? I could hear my father's voice in my head on repeat. He was often loving when he needed to be, but he could also wound me with his words.

"Use your brain. What are you? Stupid?"

Apparently, I was. Nobody prepared me for the lifelong echoes of my parents' voices in my head. Those same echoes, always putting me down, were the very reason I second guessed every decision I made. Based on the conversation with my mother that day, it seemed I was the reason justice would never be served for the crimes committed against my baby sister, other kids, and me.

That night, I laid in bed and thought about everything. I closed my eyes and tried to force myself to remember. I saw yellow tile and a white sink next to a toilet. I felt the cold tile beneath my backside. I smelled the Lysol lingering in the air. I saw a large man on top of me. I heard footsteps outside the door. I felt him climb off my small body. I heard his voice, deep and gravelly.

"Get up. Get your shoes on and hurry up."

I shifted in my bed and rolled to my side. Silently going through every memory that would push forward, a tear rolled down my cheek. This horrible man would never pay for what he did to me and that was my fault. Even at the age of twelve, I understood I was a failure.

Before I drifted to sleep, my thoughts went to my speech therapist. I thought about the time my mother dropped me off. I was crumpled in a pile of tulle ruffles on the floor of the waiting room. This gentle, loving woman picked me up and caressed my wet and matted hair away from my face.

"She'll be back. I promise. It's okay sweetie."

Her voice was so calm and soothing. I missed her. I wished I could see her again. I wanted to tell her how grateful I was for alerting my mother to Papa Joe's abuse.

"Have you noticed any behaviors at home that are out of the ordinary?"

"What do you mean?"

My mother seemed to be clueless of what my therapist was asking.

"She is withdrawn, cries more, and seems extremely frightened."

"The only thing different is her father and I are thinking about separating."

My mother stood there trying to think of anything significant. And just like that, a lightbulb seemed to go off in her head.

"She and her little sister attend a home daycare near our house. They have been going for about a year maybe."

As my therapist contemplated how to approach the subject, my mother impatiently waited.

"Have you noticed either of them acting out?"

As her eyes widened, my mother began to sob. I often would touch myself inappropriately but did not understand why or what I was doing. After the conversation with my mother on the patio, I realized this is what acting out was. I was re-enacting what was being done to me. My speech therapist was asking my mother if she had seen signs that I was being touched.

I knew my therapist was special. I wanted her to know how grateful I was for speaking up when I didn't. How grateful I was for her helping me overcome my speech delays. I wanted her to know how wonderful of a job she did. If I saw her again, I would tell her. I would not allow my meek and quiet demeanor to silence my voice again. With the thoughts of her kindness and love, I fell asleep for the first time in a long time without fear or nightmares.

# Amazing Grace

Throughout my early childhood, my Nannie made sure we went to church every Sunday. I loved singing and listening to the music from the hymnal. The first hymn I learned all the words and melody to was "Amazing Grace". The message was simple yet profound. Before knowing Christ as my savior, I was blind to the inner workings of God. When He found me broken and in despair, restoring my faith and showing me grace, I could finally see Him.

When I spent every other weekend with my daddy, we didn't go to church but that didn't mean we didn't learn about God. My daddy often spoke about God.

"You don't have to be in four walls of a church to find Jesus. You just have to go outside and look around. God is evident in everything we see."

He was right. From the beautifully painted sunsets and sunrises to the highest mountains touching the bluest skies, God's work was evident to me.

At my dad's house, his room had a large bathroom. In the bathroom, there was a garden tub. It was my favorite place to be. He would fill the water up as high as my shoulders. We had this bath toy we loved playing with in there. He was yellow and looked like a scuba diver. The legs and fins would flip and splash us as it went round and round the tub. Through the bubbles, under the water, and around my baby sister and me. We would just giggle and splash. When our bathtime was over, my daddy would pull us out one at a time. He would wrap the towel around me to dry me off and keep me warm.

"Let me check to make sure you are all squeaaaakkkyyyy clean."

His playful voice was so funny. He would run his index finger down my sternum and make a squeaking noise.

"Ssssqqqquuuuuueeeaaaakkkkk! All clean!"

If he felt like being real funny, he wouldn't make the squeaking noise. He would then take the washcloth and go back over the spot and try again. Once he made the squeaking noise, we were all clean.

My daddy used to calm my fears at night. Nighttime was the absolute worst time for me because the flashbacks, fear of being attacked, and feelings of abandonment consumed my thoughts. My baby sister and I often found ourselves in his bed rather than our own because we both would wake up scared. He would place his larger-than-life palm under our faces and scoop us close to him. We would nestle into him, one on each side. He would hum the tune of "Amazing Grace". Eventually, the tune would have lyrics. The lyrics would be different from the original hymn.

*Daddy's little babies are so sweet. Daddy's little babies are so sweet.*

He would sing this to us every night we spent at his house. Sometimes, he would change the lyrics again.

*Daddy's little babies are so smart. Daddy's little babies are so smart.*

*Daddy's little babies are so nice. Daddy's little babies are so nice.*

Looking back on those times, I realize just how loving he truly was. If he wasn't humming or singing to us to calm our fears, he was making up stories on the spot. While they varied in adventure, they kept the same theme. Every one of his stories had a moral or a lesson. My dad was strong physically, but gentle emotionally for the most part. He could be strict and intimidating; however, he could also be the gentlest giant.

When he was angry, no one stood a chance. It would come quick, sharp, and painful depending on who you were. I had often heard rumors my Pappaw was the same way. I had never witnessed it though. I had witnessed my dad's wrath several times. If we were too loud, if he couldn't control a situation or person, and other situations he determined were against him. Even though he could be angry at the snap of fingers, he still showed love in more important aspects such as when we were scared. Our vulnerability was his weakness.

Shooting, fishing, tracking animals, and the importance of gun safety were all taught to me at an early age by my dad. He was serious about it all. Sometimes, he was emotionally unavailable, but he was a tender and caring father who slayed my mental demons at nightfall and did everything he could at the time, to the best of his ability, to ensure I was taught right from wrong. No other parental figure in my life calmed my fears like my daddy.

# Fearsome Prison Blues

Fear often consumed me. Most nights, I had an indescribable need to sleep a certain way. The bed had to be positioned just right. I couldn't sleep with my back to the windows or to the door. A fear of being attacked played on repeat in my thoughts. I was not sure why I was so adamant that I was going to be attacked and stabbed while I slept. My mind would not allow me to remember.

Wetting the bed was commonplace for me. I dreamt I was on the toilet most nights and woke up drenched in bed. This had only recently stopped before we moved in with my mother and my new stepdad. I wish I knew then what I know now. Every fiber of my being had been traumatized, and at that point, I had no clue. My brain was protecting me from the horrors I had experienced by keeping the memories from me. My body, however, was not.

I grew up very wary of others. I became hypervigilant of my surroundings. I observed the demeanor of others. I paid attention to what someone focused on when spoken to.

If they let their eyes wander, my guard went up. Once, I was talking to a man while children were playing in the background. Instead of looking me in my eyes during the conversation, he stared past me at the children behind me. This type of interaction spoke volumes to me. People can tell you everything about them in their eyes without ever speaking. People up to no good often fidget. Minute details others typically would not notice, I did. Fear consumed me every hour of every day. I became enslaved to it in both mind and body.

I had a recurring nightmare from the age of six until I was about ten years old. In it, I had a bunch of bananas and Nannie wanted one. I remember one banana looking weird. Nannie took that banana. I traded her because I felt like something was off. We peeled the bananas at the same time, but something was very wrong. My banana was a rattlesnake. Once the rattlesnake slithered out of the banana, there were hundreds more suddenly at our feet. They came out of the walls. Everywhere we looked, there were rattlesnakes. I never made it out of the house before waking up. I felt like it represented something, and maybe it did.

While my mother was going to school, Nannie would drive us to meet her a few times a year. It was not always consistently a holiday, but mostly it was. Since school was out during the summer, we took at least one trip a year during that time. I assume it was easier on my mother that way. Each meeting resulted in the same outcome. We got a gift, a meal, and a hug from her, followed by tears.

When I started Kindergarten, I wore a purple coverall dress that had Garfield the cat on the front. My mother gave me that outfit for my first day of school. Nannie drove us to meet her in Cleveland, Texas because it was relatively halfway between Galveston and Nacogdoches. By then, my mother was working on her bachelor's degree in nursing. Typically, we met in Cleveland at the local McDonald's. While most families gathered around the Christmas tree, we gathered at a McDonald's for an hour exchange. These meetings kept that thread of hope alive that one day, we would be a family again. Even though my mother was often verbally abusive, I still longed for that mother-daughter bond. I craved the connection with her despite her ability to give it. I inherently believed that her mood was my responsibility. If she was happy, I must have been good. If she was angry, I was bad.

When I opened the wrapped box with such excitement, my mother was so happy.

"This is for your first day of school."

I immediately went to the bathroom and put it on. I did not want to take it off. Purple was my favorite color. I sat back down at the booth and began to eat my cheeseburger. Next thing I know, my mother is angry. *How did the switch flip so quickly this time? What did I do?* I looked down and there it was. A dot of ketchup mixed with mustard under a pickle sat there on my new purple dress. I grabbed a napkin and tried to furiously clean it off.

"Do not do that. You are making it worse. Can't you do anything right?"

The answer was always no. Nothing I ever did was right. Nothing I ever said was good enough. There I sat, frozen. Do I continue eating? Do I throw it all away? There was no right answer here. Before I knew it, we were loaded up and headed home.

"Your mother is going to let me know when she wants you both to go visit her in Galveston."

As I stared out the window, I wondered if anyone felt as alone as I did at that moment. My baby sister and I loved car rides, but this one was quiet the whole way home. Maybe if I had just sat still and ate my food slower, I wouldn't have made her angry. Maybe if I were a better child, she would love me enough to want to keep me.

The following spring, my mother wanted us to stay in Galveston with her. My baby sister and I were so excited. Our mother was too. She welcomed us into her little apartment with open arms. Her roommate, Carmen, took us to the beach while Ella finished some of her schoolwork. It was the first time I had been to the beach. It was nothing compared to what I had seen on TV. The water was dark and cold. The shoreline was compacted dirt. Carmen was really nice though and kept me from touching the washed-up jellyfish.

When we finished walking on the shore, Carmen took us walking through the downtown area of the island. It had neat little shops on each side of the street.

"This is called The Strand. Let's go find a cute shop to look in."

On our way to the shop, I noticed this man hiding around a corner. My hypervigilance began kicking in. I didn't say anything, but I did grab Carmen's hand. My eyes did not leave this man behind the corner. Our eyes locked and he motioned his finger as if trying to tell me to come to him quietly. I shook my head no and continued walking with Carmen and my baby sister.

After we finished at The Strand, we went back to the apartment. We ate dinner and were getting ready for bed. My mother made the bed up with some cute sheets with cartoon characters on them. We were tucked in and went to sleep.

Not long after, I woke up sick. Before I could even blink, I threw up all over the bed.

"Michelle! What are you doing? Why did you do that? You are old enough to throw up in the toilet. Get up!"

I didn't know what to do, so I cried. Once I started crying, she became even more enraged. She grabbed me by my shoulders and began shaking me.

"Stop crying. I just put clean sheets on this bed for you and here you are messing them up. Go to the bathroom and change your clothes."

Head down, clean clothes in hand, I toddled into the bathroom to clean myself up. Shame, guilt, sadness, and loneliness spread through me like wildfire.

"I'm sorry mommy. I didn't mean to."

Apologies did not matter. I was a burden once again. All I wanted was to make her happy. I just wanted to be held and comforted. I continued to crave for her love and affection, but instead, I continued to receive mixed signals. *Maybe, just maybe, one day she will love me. One day she will want me. One day she will be proud of me and happy with me.* Alas, I wondered if that would ever be true.

# All I want for Christmas is Stability

Our first Christmas as a new family of five was highly anticipated. My mother, stepdad, and two sisters were just as excited for it. The last time I had a Christmas morning with both sisters and a father was when I was around four years old. I can remember being by the tree and my dad wheeled my first bicycle into the living room. My parents were freshly separated. My bicycle was purple and white. I was so excited. I had never ridden one before. This memory was one of the very first memories I could ever recall that didn't start with trauma. While my stepdad couldn't replace my daddy, he still filled a wonderful role as a father-figure.

It felt like a far cry from Christmas at the Cleveland McDonald's. The final Christmas at McDonald's had been different. Nannie dropped us off with our mother. I don't know what Nannie did during that time, but I remember my mother took us to a store. There were Cabbage Patch dolls everywhere we looked. My favorite thing in the world was dolls because they were my babies. I always wanted to be a mom, and they fulfilled that desire.

I picked out my very own doll. She came with adoption papers and a bottle. Her little tuft of curly red hair sat plopped right on top of her head with a pink bow. She was my first doll that ever cried and giggled. I was enamored with her. I kept her by my side for years.

"Quit pressing her arm. I am trying to drive."

*How dare she tell me not to play with my new toy. I pressed it again.*

"Oops. It was an accident."

She glared at me through the rearview mirror. I stared out the window and smiled. The more visits we had, the angrier I got. I longed for her love and approval, but I hated goodbyes. I did not understand the reasoning behind my anger or my mother's decision to leave us behind. The less I understood, the angrier I became inside. I would hit, fight, kick, scream, and even break things when I would throw them. I had so many emotions bottled up as a child with nowhere to disperse them.

Christmas morning at the new house finally came. My baby sister and I were so excited. We tumbled out of bed and raced from our room to the living room. It was not but five feet of distance, but we clamored through the door and across the hardwood floor anyway. Staring at the tree we had all decorated, my eyes met the packages. I had never seen so many before.

Everyone was smiling. It was the happiest we had ever appeared. My mother sat on the navy-blue sectional sofa next to my stepdad. She held her hot mug of black coffee and smiled. My older sister was digging through her pile while my baby sister and I were drawn to the same thing. Our eyes widened while our jaws dropped.

Our town had a beautiful doll store downtown. The brick streets paved the way for so many glamorous storefronts, but the Bavarian Dollhouse was the only one I was interested in. Only the best of the best could afford those dolls, yet here we were with our own.

"A baby doll! A real baby doll!"

I couldn't believe we finally had one.

"There's one more gift outside. Santa couldn't get it inside the house."

When my stepdad said that we all leapt off the floor and ran down the hall, through the kitchen, and to the back patio. There it was. Standing ten feet tall with wet cement around the base. A basketball goal had been erected overnight. We couldn't wait to play.

Later that afternoon, our cousin came over with my aunt and uncle. We immediately set out for the woods and explored. My cousin found some large sticks, and with my baby sister and I, we made a teepee. In and out, around and under we went through the sticks of the teepee. Afterwards, we rode bikes over and around the mounds of dirt in the front yard. Playing with my cousin and my baby sister always made me happy. My mother's brother and his wife had been a recurring part of our upbringing with Nannie. We spent time with them every summer. I loved helping with my aunt's home daycare.

"I'm going to have my own daycare one day."

My aunt would smile. She loved our visits. My uncle did too. He was strict, but he was also goofy. We always enjoyed staying with them. When we weren't helping with the daycare, we were in the backyard swimming in their pool. I couldn't swim because of my chronic ear infections and ear tubes, but I flapped in the water regardless. My cousin, my baby sister, and I were always close, but this would be one of the last times I would see them for many years. The reason why depended on who you asked. Mental illness was not something we heard about, but between my uncle and mother, it existed. The effects of mental illness would plague our family for years to come.

# Freedom Isn't Free

Mental illness, like sexual abuse, was not a discussion anyone was willing to have. In fact, whether it was said or not, it was implied not to speak about it.

*Nobody wants to hear about that, Michelle.*

The visit from my aunt, uncle, and cousin that Christmas was the last time we had contact with them for many years. According to my mother, Uncle James was paranoid about a mug of coffee she brought to him. Supposedly, he felt like she was poisoning him with the coffee. After an argument, they didn't see each other again.

My uncle had paranoid schizophrenia. My mother had bipolar disorder. The difference between the two of them was very simple. One sought professional help while the other denied its existence. I will always commend Uncle James for his courage in seeking help and following through.

Bipolar ripped through my household like a tornado, leaving despair and sadness in its wake. Jobs, money, and relationships eventually failed. My mother lost her job at the hospital and had to find work outside of Nacogdoches. The bridges she continued to burn kept adding up. Living with her was like riding a rollercoaster with no end in sight. When her mood was good, she was great. When her mood was down, she was awful.

Losing the new house was hard. We packed everything up and moved to a rental home. It didn't have a backyard to play in because of the thick piney woods that backed up to the property. It was pink on the outside and had a beautiful front porch. When you walked in the front door, you knew you were home. It looked and felt like a time capsule from the Victorian era. The hardwood floors had been restored throughout the home.

At the back of the house, one end had the sunroom while the other end had a little hallway, or passageway as I called it, leading to the master bedroom. Each bedroom had floor to ceiling double doors. Our older sister took the front room next to the bathroom. My baby sister and I took the room that backed up to the passageway. Our bedroom had window cut outs that faced the passageway but had no glass. Just two open squares.

One night, my baby sister and I sat up playing video games. Before we knew it, our mother barged in.

"I can see the lights from your room down the hall into my room. Go to bed."

We turned the game off and slid in bed. After waiting a few minutes, we grabbed two black pillowcases and some thumb tacks. We were determined to cover those damn windows because Mario Kart and Wave Race were calling our names.

Anytime she was home, you never knew what version you were going to get. I could almost time her moods. If she woke up in a silly and playful mood, we had to take advantage of it. If we had any documents needing to be signed for school, now was the time. If there were any activities we wanted to attend, we had to ask during those moments. Unfortunately, there were more bad moods than good. If she woke up silently, we knew to stay out of her way. If she woke up yelling, we immediately busied ourselves with chores. Everyone in the house was constantly on pins and needles. There was no stopping the emotional rollercoaster of someone diagnosed with bipolar disorder who refused to seek treatment.

I really liked my stepdad. He always included us and made us feel important. The best memory of our family together was lunch after church on Sundays. We would come home, and he would make Velveeta and Rotel dip with chips. He tried so hard to make their marriage work. Nothing was ever good enough for my mother.

During middle school, there was a "shadow a parent at work" day. I chose to follow Curtis, my stepdad. He was making cabinets in the shop that was attached to our garage. The shop he built was larger than the double car garage and had a half bathroom. He kept all his tools and work horses in there. I was so excited to shadow him. I even packed a sack lunch and acted like I wasn't at home, rather, I was at work. He taught me about corners, measurements, and angles. By the end of the day, we made a cabinet together.

In the new pink rental we moved to, we were gathered in the living room with Curtis. My mother wasn't there because she had to work. When she got home, they started arguing.

"Why is it I work all night, three nights in a row and I come home to you getting to spend time with my girls? You all are just having the time of your lives eating pizza and watching TV while I am working. Just using all my money. You are lazy."

My mother knew how to throw verbal punches. Sadly, Curtis knew it was not a fight he was winning, so he retreated. He ended up sleeping on the couch until the end of their marriage.

One morning in the pink house, my mother asked me to get her socks from the top drawer in her dresser. I opened the dresser but there was something on top of the socks, keeping the drawer from opening all the way. It was a folded newspaper ad. I opened it up and saw where there were young people circled on the pages. They were teenage girls modeling bras. I ran it to my mother. I couldn't understand what I was seeing.

"What is this?"

As she fumbled through the pages, I waited for her response.

"That bastard! I knew he was acting strange around you girls."

I was even more confused at this point. He had never acted strange around us.

"What are you talking about, mom?"

"You don't worry about anything. I am divorcing him. This is the last straw."

When he came home from work that day, all hell broke loose. The arguing and the fighting continued through the night. Just when I thought she was done, she came around again. It was one of the worst verbal fighting matches I had witnessed. There was nothing he could say or do. Nothing mattered anymore. He conceded and the packing began. We were moving. They were divorcing. There was no turning back.

After a year in the pink house, they were finished, and we were uprooted again. My mother found herself separated and on the cusp of divorce for a second time in her life after less than three years of marriage. She had nobody to blame but herself. Unmedicated bipolar disorder is no treat. I knew this personally because years into my adulthood, I was diagnosed as well. The difference was I was willing to see a doctor.

At the start of my freshman year, I felt like things were going smoothly at home after my mother's divorce. I was starting high school, my baby sister was starting middle school, and my oldest sister had graduated and moved out on her own. My mother was getting back on her feet financially and everything was smooth sailing. I was in choir while my baby sister was in band. School kept us busy while our mother worked her standard night shifts at the other local hospital. It was getting better, until it wasn't.

In the almost four years since I had moved in with my mother, we had moved a total of seven times. Nothing was stable. When things felt unsure, my anxiety took over. This would spiral into guilt, shame, sadness, and anger. When I was angry, I had no control anymore. I hit, kicked, screamed, and talked back. When I hit, I was a danger to others and myself.

These fits of rage and physical violence started when I was little. Too little to understand how to handle the adult-like position Papa Joe put me in as well as the position of holding onto my secrets so as not to upset those around me.

My baby sister took the brunt of my rage. She always had. Anytime I felt like I was losing control of any situation, I fought. If my baby sister even uttered a word during my inner turmoil, I took it out on her. Even when she didn't upset me on purpose, my anger and rage would win my inner battle of right versus wrong. I did many years of damage to the one person in my life who loved me the most.

I often wonder if I had been able or encouraged to talk about what happened to me, if I could have learned better ways to handle the anger and various emotions I had to deal with silently. There are plenty of reasons why adults failed both of us in this situation, but I fully grasp the totality of pain and torment I caused my baby sister. I will regret the physical, emotional, and mental pain I caused her for the rest of my life.

By the time I was fourteen, my physical outbursts had subsided for the most part. I met my future husband at the same time my mother was preparing for divorce. He was funny, kind, and caring. His green eyes melted my soul. I felt like I found my missing piece. My baby sister loved him too. When he would get off work at night, he would stop by sometimes and watch "I Love Lucy" reruns with us. He was two years ahead of me, so he graduated from high school before I did. When he left for college, my world shattered. I felt abandoned. The day he left, I felt the same way as I had felt the day my mother drove off into the sunset to start her new life without me. Damaged, unworthy, unlovable.

It took two years for him to get through school while I finished high school. They were extremely hard and emotionally draining. Long distance relationships are not for the weak, but we made it. I graduated school and moved out of my mother's as soon as I could. The last order she gave me before I moved out was at my graduation lunch with my future in-laws.

"Now that you have graduated, pack your things and get out."

And with that, I did. Instead of her leaving me behind, I left her, and it felt great. I was finally free. Or so I thought.

# 8

# Plains, Trains, and North Dakota

After graduating high school, I moved in with Stephen and his parents. Three months later, the twin towers collapsed. I looked at the love of my life with fear in my eyes. He looked determined. Four months later, he joined the Air Force after ringing in the new year. We made it halfway through basic training before I mailed him a letter with life-changing news. I was pregnant. By the time he received the letter and was able to make a phone call, I had already confirmed with doctors that I was several weeks along. He was ecstatic. I was scared to death. Here he was on Lackland Air Force Base going through basic training, and I had to tell everyone I was pregnant alone. Those conversations went about as well as expected. My older sister was immediately supportive and reassuring. We hadn't been very close but my baby in my belly changed that. My baby sister was happy, but she told me she would be elated if I would let her tell our mother. I did. That's the one person I didn't want to deal with. I told

Stephen's mom first. She was the one person I was most comfortable talking to.

"Everything is going to be alright. We will take care of you. Don't worry."

Her words gave me hope. Hope that everything would be alright. Keeping the baby was never a question. This baby was precious and a miracle. My little miracle. She or he would always be loved by us. Whether he and I made it or not. I laid my hand on my belly that night and fell asleep dreaming of the little baby I was going to have.

Before long, everyone knew we were expecting, but not everyone was supportive. My mother finally called me.

"Well, you made it longer than I thought you would. I figured you would have ended up pregnant in high school."

Rolling my eyes, I quickly finished that conversation and hung up. There was no use in arguing with her. Nothing she said would change my situation. I was having this baby. My next call was to Stephen's grandmother. That went just as well as my mother's conversation.

"How could you let this happen?"

*Oh yes. I completely let this happen all on my own.*

I quickly passed the phone off to my future father-in-law. Whether anyone else was happy about this baby or not, I did not care. I had always wanted to be a mom. Stephen and I had many conversations between us about our wants and desires in life. He wanted to go to the Air Force to work with the computer systems for the missile sites. He was beginning that dream. I wanted to be a mom and work with children. Despite the nay-sayers, we were ready for the challenge ahead.

After he graduated from boot camp, he was shipped off to California for Tech School. Unfortunately, he was given the bad news that due to his credit score, he could not attain the clearance needed for the job he wanted. Determination for a life together far outweighed the disappointment of not attaining his desired job. I flew to California, and we got married. With our baby growing in my belly, we wed at the courthouse. I flew back to Texas two days later proudly wearing his last name.

In June of that year, we said our goodbyes to our families and set off in his 1985 Grand Marquis. The drive to Minot, North Dakota was going to take twenty-five hours. We broke it up into three days. The drive was going by fast until we hit South Dakota. There was nothing but corn fields and open skies. Not a tree in sight. Coming from the piney woods of East Texas, barren plains as far as the eye could see was incredible. With my swollen bare feet on the dash, we kept moving.

On day three, we arrived in Minot, North Dakota. The town of Minot was such a cute town nestled in a bowl. They called it the valley. It was the definition of a Hallmark movie. Downtown Minot was a few blocks from the main highway. The worst crime reported was people writing hot checks. The main highway through the middle of the town was Highway 83, also known as Broadway. When we first entered Minot, we took in all the sights we could. On our left, there was an A&W Root Beer shop. On the right, there was a store called Menard's. After what felt like fifty-seven traffic lights, we finally came to the edge of town. Once we rolled through the final traffic light, we headed fifteen miles north toward the base. The road was just as barren as the fields on each side of it. Every now and again there were fields of giant golden sunflowers.

"Why are there so many sunflowers?"

Stephen grabbed my hand and smiled. He gave me a little giggle before answering.

"Baby, they use the sunflowers for seeds and oil. I bet we will also see tons of corn fields."

I continued looking out the window, because aside from California, I had never been out of Texas. I loved seeing the different landscapes along our drive for the last few days. We finally arrived at Minot Air Force Base and it was so foreign to me. It was like being on a compound that was heavily guarded all the time. A wall encompassed the whole base. We were searched at the gate by guards before we could enter. Once we arrived at the address provided, a tall man with black hair came out and greeted us.

"Are you the new recruit?"

"Yessir! I am reporting for duty."

The guy laughed and looked at us up and down.

"You're from the south. You must be."

We both laughed with him and smiled. We hadn't even thrown out our stereotypical "y'all" yet. Not even a "howdy". Stephen shook his head and snickered.

"Texas, actually."

"Where is your cowboy hat?"

I rolled my eyes and laughed.

"We didn't bring our boots either."

I went back to the car while Stephen went inside to get everything together. Shortly after, we were taken to our temporary living facility, which is the military's version of a hotel. After we unloaded the car, we took photos of the sun setting with not a tree in sight. This was going to be the beginning of a wonderful life.

# Pink Skies in His Eyes

Stephen and I fell in love with Minot rather quickly, despite any feelings of missing home. It was a new start to life for both of us. The day we arrived in Minot, Stephen had to put us on the waitlist for housing on base. The wait for a house was long, so we found an apartment downtown. However, it wouldn't be ready for another month. The new airman we met our first day on base graciously invited us into his home with his wife. They were our first friends. It turned out Stephen would be working in the mechanic shop with Bo. His wife worked off base, but she was just as wonderful as he was.

Once we moved into our new apartment downtown, we prepared for the arrival of our baby. I was eight months pregnant when I started seeing blood.

"This can't be happening."

"It's okay, baby. I will get you to the hospital and get you checked out."

With that, we loaded up and drove the two blocks to Trinity Health. My anxiety and fear consumed me.

"What if the move hurt the baby? What if I did something wrong?"

He put his arm around my shoulders and his other hand on my belly and looked me directly in the eyes.

"Our baby is going to be okay. You did nothing wrong."

Once they triaged me and had me in a room, they brought in an ultrasound machine. Waiting to hear the heartbeat felt like an eternity.

"I'm going to put this gel on your belly. It may be cold."

Tears started welling up. The worry I had over this little life inside me was already slamming into me, and he or she wasn't even here yet.

"Do you want to know the sex of your baby?"

I wiped my tears and nodded with a huge smile. Stephen grabbed my hand.

"When I was in basic training, I prayed for this baby. When I looked up, the sky was all shades of pink. This is a girl."

I loved that story even more each time he told it to me.

"While I was waiting for an interview with Wal-Mart, I was praying about my pregnancy. After I prayed about it, I looked up. Right there in front of me was a mylar balloon rack of different balloons you could choose from. My eyes went right to the one that said 'Congratulations, it's a girl.'"

Both of us had our own signs of what we were having. We both waited with anticipation.

"I am seventy-five percent sure this is a girl, and she has one healthy heartbeat."

The relief we both felt filled the room. Our baby girl was healthy, safe, and extremely loved.

# Metamorphosis

Our first winter came just before our precious girl arrived. The white crystals fell so softly around us. We were awestruck. East Texas didn't get snow like this. In fact, it rarely got cold enough to bundle up. Minot was different. We were not prepared for this experience. The first week of constant snowfall was so beautiful.

By week two, we were over it. Snowplows traveled daily to clear the roads, while dump trucks dropped sand behind them. Black ice was dangerous stuff. That is what they called ice that re-iced itself repeatedly until it looked like black glass. If you hit it fast enough, your car instantly lost control.

Between the winds, snowfall, and snowplows, the snow-drifts piled upwards of ten feet tall. While it was breathtakingly beautiful, it was also extremely monotonous. If the winds blew hard enough and the temperature dropped low enough, the power would go out. Based on the road conditions, you may or may not be able to leave your home.

One morning, I woke up extremely early. I was mid-pee when I realized what was happening. I ran to the bathroom. I sat on the toilet and released my bladder.

*Wait. If I am peeing now, then why am I wet?*

"Stephen! Wake up!"

Excitement and panic raced through me simultaneously.

"What's wrong?"

Barely awake, he saw me sitting there with drenched bottoms.

"I think my water broke."

We immediately called the hospital and loaded the car. It was baby time!

We arrived at the hospital by 5:15 a.m. Exactly twelve hours later, Flora was born. Her hair was the color of a shiny new penny. With both of us being brunette, we were stunned. However, my husband had auburn flecks in his beard when he grew it out, and red hair ran in the maternal side of my family. She was six pounds of beautiful perfection. Thirty minutes after her arrival, I spiked a fever and passed out.

The next morning, I woke up and looked around my hospital room.

"Where's the baby?"

My doting husband had been asleep in the horrendous chair in the corner.

"You're awake! I'll go get her!"

Within minutes, a nurse rushed in followed by my husband. After answering questions about where I was and who I was, they deemed me safe enough to hold my sweet daughter. Apparently, the epidural caused me to spike a fever and pass out after giving birth. Flora was worth it. She was worth everything I had ever been through to get to this moment. Our baby girl represented love and rebirth.

My mother sent a check for the nursery furniture several days prior to Flora's arrival. Stephen and Bo had put it together just hours before we brought her home. Her room was decorated in shades of blue, yellow, and green. My heart swelled with happiness at the little family we had created.

# Ain't No Sunshine When He's Gone

Once we were settled in at home, I sat down at the kitchen table to write a thank you letter to my mother for the baby furniture. Something I learned quickly with her when it came to gifts is that there were always strings attached. In fact, gifts must have been her love language because it's all she spoke. Anytime I tried to tell her she hurt my feelings I would receive a gift instead of an apology. If she needed something from me, there was a bribe with a gift. When she wanted to be praised for being such a great mother, there were gifts. The gifts didn't have to be extravagant. She often chose gifts based on my interests.

On the flip side of that, if we ever needed any money and asked for it, she held it over our heads. If we didn't concede to her demands, she flipped through her mental rolodex of monetary help to find the best one to manipulate us with. If we didn't thank her profusely, we were called names.

Through all the ups and downs, I still wanted her. I still wanted to feel wanted by my mother.

I loved music growing up. I sang in choir all through school. My mother used to bribe me with CDs from the store if I would go with her. I went every time. Miss out on a new CD? Not this chick! I learned quickly that when she was in a good mood and wanted something from me, I was able to ask for something I needed or wanted at that time. Manipulative? Maybe, but I considered it survival in her home.

"You are such a manipulative child."

I felt like I was always crying too much, but it was also a lie I believed for years.

Her words always cut deep, but I couldn't let her know it hurt.

"You are too sensitive. You cry too much. Maybe you just need a nap."

While others my age were agitated at themselves for having a song stuck in their head, I had my mother's words stuck on repeat in mine. It was sad and maddening at the same time. My sisters received even more abuse from her than I did. It will never be lost on me that I was treated better, and I held that guilt for decades. They didn't deserve it, but I didn't either. We were just kids.

*I will not treat my kids like she did.*

I licked the envelope and addressed it to her. Flora was ready for her first tub bath. Stephen ran her bath while I undressed her. I carried her to the bathroom and placed her tiny body into the infant bathtub. Her little eyes looked all around. Such a big world for a little girl. I started bathing her and started crying. Stephen didn't understand. How could he?

"I can't bathe her. You're going to have to bathe her."

I ran out of the bathroom and collected myself. A few minutes later, he was drying her off and getting her dressed. He brought her to me, and I held her in my arms.

"What happened in there?"

I was finally calm enough to talk about it.

"I am scared to bathe her because I am scared others will think I am hurting her."

"You wouldn't hurt her. What are you talking about?"

I took a deep breath and forged ahead.

"Many people assume that molested children will grow up and molest children too. I don't want anyone thinking I would do that to her."

He wrapped his arm around me and rubbed Flora's face with his other hand.

"I would never think that about you. Flora is safe with you."

I took comfort in his words and was so grateful for him. When we were dating, we would lay on a grassy hill at the football track. Our hometown had a decent-sized college with a beautiful stadium. We would lay on the hill, staring up at the stars while talking about our future. Contrary to others' beliefs, we genuinely spent our alone time immersed in our plans.

When Flora was ten months old, our base house came available. We moved from our downtown apartment that already held so many memories into a much larger home. We now lived in a four-plex. I had never seen or heard of those until Minot. It's like a duplex, only there are four units with two garages on each side of the building. When you walked through the front door, you were in a small foyer. To the right, there was the living room/dining room combo. To the left, there was a set of stairs leading up. Straight ahead was the kitchen. Upstairs, there were two bedrooms and a bathroom. In the kitchen, there was a door. When you opened that door, it led downstairs to a basement. Hardwood floors were throughout the unit. This was our new home.

Eventually, I had to get a job. I didn't want to work, but I needed to work. I applied at the childcare center on base and got the job. When she was fourteen months old, I dropped Flora off with a friend on base and cried the whole way to work. After getting my thoughts together and wiping my face, I went inside. Meeting new people had always been a challenge for me. Once I warmed up though, I really enjoyed my new coworkers. Within a month, they had a spot available for Flora to attend. I spent my lunch breaks checking on her. This continued for a year until I switched from working at the center to working at home. I started an at home daycare on base and continued that for the next three years.

After being in the new house for a year, my husband would be handed his first deployment. A deployment is where the military member goes somewhere else, such as overseas, for longer than a few months. His first deployment was to Kuwait. He was gone five months. He called every chance he was able to. Flora never forgot who her daddy was. Every time the phone rang, she would come running.

"Daddy?"

I would nod whether it was him or not. If not, she would pout and run off to her toys. If it was him, she would drop everything she was doing to get on the phone. Their relationship was the best. His comedic behavior coupled with her thirst for life made them inseparable.

When he finally arrived back home, we decided to try to expand our family. Flora was almost three years old, and we felt it would be the perfect time. God's timing and my timing were two different things. It would be two more years before I could become pregnant again.

"Your daughter is a miracle. With Polycystic Ovary Syndrome, you are extremely lucky to even have her."

The specialist reiterated that new treatments may or may not work. I tried the pills and the shots to no avail. We even considered adoption. During one of my latest scans, they saw a polyp on my fallopian tube. After having a D & C to biopsy it, they returned to tell me there was nothing there.

"It must've been a shadow. You are just fine."

I went home to recover from the procedure and let the anesthesia wear off. A few days later, we had news.

"I am being deployed to Iraq."

My heart sank. Iraq was not as bad as Afghanistan, but it was still bad. We were a rollercoaster of emotions for a few days. Less than a month later, he was packed and ready to go. This deployment was supposed to only last six months. I was grateful. My baby sister's husband was in the Army. He was deployed for eighteen months at a time. I couldn't imagine. I was grateful that I didn't have to.

One month after he left, I received a phone call from him. I spoke briefly so Flora could talk to him. This deployment was a little harder than the first one because she was a little older. She missed him. We talked as long as we could and finally hung up. The time between phone calls depended on him. When I had news, I had to wait until he could call again. It wouldn't be until the next phone call that I could tell him we were pregnant again.

# The Big Bad Wolf in Sheep's Clothing

By the time Stephen returned home from deployment, I was nearing my eighth month of pregnancy. Our second daughter was set to be born in October of that year. After much consideration, we decided to move back to Texas to be closer to family. This meant Stephen would not re-enlist in the military, but he would join the reserves instead.

During his months long tour in Iraq, my mother and I had become closer through phone calls. She and her current boyfriend had been together for seven years. They had recently bought a home together in McKinney, Texas. Both were nurses and had met in Tyler. Their relationship began while I was in my senior year of high school. There were no introductions until almost two years into their relationship. She didn't disclose we even existed until then. While the choices she made throughout our lives weren't ideal, I still longed for a relationship with her. I still craved a mother's love.

After Lea was born, we moved to McKinney to start anew. We were so grateful for the friends we met in Minot, but we were ready to be home in Texas. Months of planning had been done to ensure the trip would be smooth for the girls. As soon as we arrived in McKinney, my mother ran to us in the driveway.

"You look awful."

"Nice to see you too. I had a baby six weeks ago."

Sadly, our time living in their house before our first purchased home was ready was volatile. When she wasn't commenting on my appearance, she was fighting with her boyfriend. At this rate, they were common law husband and wife. He had started a carpet cleaning business. He also added a solar screen business to the mix. My husband was partners with him in both ventures.

Our first house we ever purchased was a beautiful two-story home on Dalhart Trail. When we walked through the front door, were immediately drawn to the open space. The dining area ran into the living room. There was a beautiful fireplace in the corner of the living area. Glancing around the room, I imagined family traditions here. It was perfect. To the right of the entryway, there was a half bathroom. There was also a staircase to our right. Around the corner was the kitchen. The kitchen was large with tons of counter space. I could imagine cooking and baking in there so easily. It also had a breakfast nook. Just off the breakfast nook, you had the laundry room that was combined with the large pantry area. I had never seen so many shelves for groceries before.

Upstairs, the master bedroom was immediately to the right. It was such a wonderful space. It was so big that we could put a seating area if we wanted to. The bathroom was one of my favorite spaces. I could see myself relaxing in the tub that was next to the enclosed shower. This was more than I could ever dream of.

One of the three bedrooms, aside from ours, was less than five feet from us. As you moved past the bedroom, you came to an upstairs living room. I couldn't wait to set up the girls' play area there. I could just imagine the two girls playing there together with matching kid-sized chairs. The last two bedrooms completed the upstairs along with their bathroom. Flora picked the last bedroom, directly across from the bathroom. Lea took the room next to Flora. The empty bedroom would be an office.

After having Lea, my mental health was declining so I went to see a doctor. I was diagnosed with bipolar disorder and anxiety. I called my mother to let her know. I don't know that I expected anything worth listening to, but I felt compelled to tell her anyway.

"The doctor said I have bipolar disorder and anxiety. He also made sure I knew it was hereditary."

She scoffed at the thought.

"You didn't get it from me."

Denial was always her favorite deflection.

"Either way, I am starting on medications and will not give up until something helps."

She didn't have to say another word. Her scoffing and chuckles said enough. It wasn't a battle I was willing to fight. Throughout my teenage years, I felt I was two people. My mother told me horrible things one moment, but encouraging things the next. Sometimes, I felt like I was inherently good, but other times, I felt like I was evil. Like something was wrong with me. I hoped the medicine would eventually help this feeling.

We decided to spend our first Thanksgiving in our hometown. Most of our families still lived there, so we felt it was the most reasonable option. Neither of our grandparents were traveling. Stephen's parents had just bought a new home too. While we were there that Thanksgiving, we helped them as much as we could to unpack. His parents were always so good to me. It infuriated my mother.

The day after Thanksgiving, I received a text message from my mother.

*I hope you all die in a car wreck. You never spend holidays with us.*

I was helping my mother-in-law when the message came through. She must have been able to see the hurt on my face.

"What's wrong?"

I tried not to cry. Now was not the time or place to be a cry-baby.

"My mother texted me. She hopes my family and I die in a car wreck."

She shook her head and hugged me. This woman didn't birth me, but she sure took me in as her own. I was so grateful to God for her. Her patience and gentleness never wavered. I pushed my mother out of my mind as much as I could. *Why does she always have to inflict pain on me when I am happy?*

In the moments of love and affection, she could be so wonderful. I could see glimpses of joy and contentment in those rare, yet fleeting times. I often wondered why I craved her love and attention despite knowing full well it didn't last. I think deep down, I held onto the good parts while making excuses for the bad. *She had a long night. Her job is stressful.*

*She's a single mother. I caused that. I didn't heed her warning. I didn't pay attention to the cues. I was overly emotional. I was too loud. I was disobedient. I was too much. Whatever too much may be, whether it consisted of too much volume, too much crying, too much neediness, too much attention, too much pressure, or even too much love.* Regardless of my thoughts and feelings, I had been taught that her needs and feelings must come first. I did my best to comply.

Our first Christmas in the house was magical. We were able to host family gatherings with people we hadn't seen in years. Friends and family were much closer now. Stephen and I were overjoyed to be home. It just felt right. Until it didn't.

Living in McKinney had its fair share of ups and downs. The six years in Minot helped us repair our credit and improve our quality of life. Six months after moving to McKinney, we were financially struggling. Our credit plummeted while we tried to stay afloat. I was diagnosed with bipolar disorder and started a battle of medication. After trying five different ones, the doctor finally prescribed a combination that worked. I no longer found myself angry at the little things. I was able to handle stressors easier. Change wasn't as hard for me, which was good because during our second Christmas there, we found out we were expecting our third child.

In my final month of that pregnancy, the doctor and I chose an induction date. I was four days out from the date when our lives completely changed. After laying Lea down for a nap, I laid in my bed. I wanted to read a few chapters in a book I was immersed in. After a few minutes, I went downstairs to check on Flora and get some water. When I made it down the stairs, she was standing in the living room with her pants down. My anxiety immediately pulsed through me.

"Sweetheart, what are you doing?"

Flora hurriedly pulled her pants up and sat on the couch. She put her blanket over her head. I sat down next to her. Gathering my thoughts, I knew I had to proceed very carefully so as not to lead her to any answers.

"What were you doing baby?"

She sat silently under her blanket. I rubbed her back before asking another question.

"Where did you learn that from?"

She slowly moved the blanket off her face.

"Peepaw."

There was only one person she called Peepaw. I picked up my phone and immediately called my husband. He was on lunch, but I told him to come straight home. When he arrived, I told him what she said, and we called 911. We didn't know who else to call in this situation. After the officer arrived, he took my statement and made a report to CPS. I may have let my perpetrator get away scot-free, but there was no way I was letting that happen to her.

# 13

# When a Volcano Meets a Tornado

Everything seemed to happen so fast after we made the report. I immediately called my older sister. Her kids always spent a week during the summer with our mother. No matter how careful I was, I missed the signs of a predator. We all did. From the time Flora could talk, I taught her about her body. Even when she attended daycare, I checked her during bath time for any signs of abuse. I had been so hypervigilant, but in the end, I felt it was all for nothing.

My sister confirmed with her two children that they were not harmed in any way. With a huge sigh of relief, I needed to call my mother at work. There was no way she could go home to her granddaughter's abuser. I knew without a doubt that because my mother had taken me out of my abusive situation, she wasn't going to stand for this. I grabbed my phone and called the hospital she worked at.

"I need to speak to Ella."

After waiting for a few minutes, she was on the line.

"What is going on? Why are you calling me at work?"

I knew she sounded annoyed, but I couldn't let this go.

"You can't go home tonight. Just come straight to us."

"What do you mean?"

"Your husband molested Flora."

Not only did I hear her sigh of agitation, I also felt it.

"I cannot deal with this right now. I am at work. Do not call back up here."

The line went dead. I felt my knees buckle as my heart sank. All those feelings of shame, guilt, abandonment, and fear welled up inside me and poured down my cheeks. As I lay in a heap, I was transported back to that office floor where my therapist always picked me up so gently. I wish she was here now. I quickly wiped my eyes and picked myself up. I couldn't break down in front of Flora. I had to be strong.

The next two days were filled with immediate responsibilities. My husband and I put the deposit down on an apartment for my mother. My older sister drove the four-hour trip to help get our mother's belongings from the house. She was the only one he allowed inside to gather things. While the cops mediated, Peter kept spewing his vitriol at me. I was unbothered. I was in full-on mama bear mode.

On the eve of my induction, both of my sisters and my mother stayed with us. The four of us women sat on the couch talking about the arrival of the newest baby. In the midst of the utter destruction of our lives, she had almost been forgotten about. Looks can be deceiving. We were so excited for her arrival. Flora and Lea were ready for baby Rose. Her impending arrival was the calm we needed before the next round of storms.

The next morning, we loaded up for the hospital so we could begin the process of welcoming our third little girl. While we had always hoped to have a boy, we were still just as enamored with the thought of another girl. All three of our girls were given to us by God. That afternoon, Rose was born. She was just as perfect as her older sisters.

Once Rose was born, my mother came and held her briefly. I was so excited for her to see Rose because this is the first of my children she was there for. Within minutes, she was gone to continue setting up her new apartment. Since Rose and I received a clean bill of health, we were able to go home the next day. We continued to settle into our new normal, but struggled for the next three months to make ends meet.

When Rose was three months old, my mother watched Flora and Lea for me. Rose had her checkup. When I returned from the appointment, my mother had Lea in her lap while Flora had her head down to the ground. My mother always made it clear Lea was her favorite. I immediately felt something was wrong.

"Flora, what is wrong?"

Before she could even respond, my mother was talking for her.

"She's just upset because she isn't getting her way."

I knew my child better than that.

"What did you do to my child?"

Anger welled up inside me. It's one thing to make me feel negative about myself, but it's a whole new ballgame when it's my child.

"I just told her that if she wanted to go to the family day on base for your husband, she would kill her baby sister because of H1N1."

I saw red. I saw black. I saw every color and every shade in-between. I was consumed with pure rage. Flora must have mentioned to her the upcoming event the base was having for reservists' families. She had been looking forward to going. With the news broadcasting a new virus sweeping the nation, my mother the nurse expected my seven-year-old to know about it. Obviously, Ella decided we weren't going. We hadn't even decided if we were going or not. I knew she favored Lea over Flora, but this was way out of line. My mind was reeling.

"Get out. Get out of my house. Don't ever say something like that to my child, let alone any child. What is wrong with you?"

As she was getting ready to leave, she turned back toward me and pointed her bony finger at me.

"Your daughter has a demon inside her. She lied about Peter. She caused me to lose my home and my hot tub. She made me lose my pool. You made him get charged with a felony. I am going to have you charged with one too."

After a few choice words from me to her, I slammed the door and held my children. Memories of how cold my mother could be ransacked my mind. The only thing she cared about was her precious image. Her image of being a wonderful and nurturing mother. The best mother a nurse could be. My dreams of reconnecting with my mother and making her proud of me dissipated before me. Everyone was crying. My world was crumbling around me, and I had no way to fix it.

# As I Walked Through the Valleys

By November of 2009, we packed up our home and moved back to Nacogdoches. Three months of struggling for work and drowning in bills forced our hand. The house ended up foreclosed, my car was repossessed not long after, and our in-laws had to take us in. Thankfully, we both had jobs lined up. Stephen was going to work at a local motorhome company while I was going to be working nights at a call center.

My mother began telling anyone who would listen that we stole money from them, lied about Peter, and that I taught Flora how to touch herself and what to say. Broken wasn't the right term. Devastated was close. Absolutely destroyed was even more accurate. My own mother poisoned my extended family against me. That wasn't the worst of it. My Nannie said I wasn't allowed to see her. She still loved me and called every now and again, but I was not allowed to visit. My mother had convinced her this was all out war, and I was the enemy.

We enrolled Flora in school, moved into a rental, and picked up our shattered pieces as best we could. My sweet, outgoing, loving husband became a shell of himself. He was scared to get close to Flora because he didn't want to cause her any flashbacks of what had happened to her. He didn't want to physically or emotionally spark any memories of her trauma. So, he became less emotionally available while I became angry inside. I shut everyone out. I started turning to alcohol.

I believed alcohol would numb the pain; that it would make all my problems disappear. When I drank, I ignored the pain, the memories, the thoughts, the flashbacks, and the voice in my head. The voice of my mother telling me I was manipulative, too needy, and too emotionally unpredictable. By drinking, I could emulate a happy, outgoing, and humorous version of me that I merely wished I truly was. Unfortunately, I continuously put myself in situations that could have potentially harmed me. Situations that could have torn my marriage apart. I didn't care.

The loving husband I once knew turned into a recluse. He no longer craved adventure. He stayed to himself. When he was home, he was immersed in computer games. When we were alone, we had mundane conversations about things that, looking back, didn't matter. We no longer communicated. We no longer connected. His anger toward Peter was nothing compared to the anger he felt toward himself. Both of us suffered, but instead of working together to heal, he used gaming, and I used alcohol.

During my work shifts, I would find myself in the parking lot drinking vodka-laced soda or whatever I could disguise in a fast-food cup. On my lunch breaks, I would run to the corner store and grab a Four Loko. Once I finished it, I would go back to work like nothing happened. I was happy at work. I made people laugh. If I didn't tell them what was going on, they didn't know. My mask was flawless on the outside. Inside, I was in turmoil. In a matter of months, I had lost my mother, my grandmother, my aunts, uncles, cousins, and eventually, my baby sister. Peter and Ella convinced them all that me, my husband, and our kids were the enemy.

Once we moved into the rental house, strange things started occurring. I made it home one morning after my shift and pulled into the driveway. I needed to go to the store. I called a friend to go with me. On my way to pick her up, I saw an animal run across the road. It was dark at 2:30 a.m., so I wasn't sure what it was. It crossed the street and waited on the opposite side. As I passed it, I looked right at it because I didn't understand what I was seeing. Its piercing dark eyes followed my gaze. I felt extremely uneasy. It wasn't a wild hog, although they were prominent there. Given its size, I thought it was a large dog or small deer. I was wrong. What I saw was a demon. Its hairless black body stood around three feet high while its gargoyle-like head was above that. Nobody believed me, but that's what it was. I needed to change how I was living, but I was stubborn.

Six months after moving to the rental, we moved again. This time, we moved to a smaller and more affordable rental across town. My older sister was the only immediate family communicating with me. Now, she was on the next street over. When I thought back on my childhood, I realized just how strong she had been as a child. She had had the weight of the world on her shoulders because my mother placed it there. Lyn picked up what my mother neglected. Just like she took care of me growing up, she continued taking care of me after the decimation of my family. I would never be able to repay her for the support, strength, and courage she shared with me and taught me.

As the children grew, Rose struggled. At eighteen-months of age, the doctor referred her to speech therapy. I chose the office my speech therapist opened all those years ago. I turned my paperwork in for her and spoke to the front desk.

"Can you please let the owner know I stopped by? I would like to get in touch with her."

Later that day, my phone rang. I don't know what I expected to come from reaching out, but I knew I needed to.

"Is this Michelle?"

Suddenly, my face lit up. Her voice, although older, was still the same calming voice from so long ago. I wanted to tell her so many things, but I didn't. What if I was too needy? What if I was all those terrible things my mother said I was? What if she didn't even remember me?

"Yes, this is she."

That phone call changed the whole trajectory of my life. We started talking regularly and got together frequently. We walked beautiful trails together and went to the gym. We often just sat together talking about life. Mainly what I had been, and was currently, going through. She invited me to church. I hadn't been to church in years. I had always felt God and prayed to Him despite not going to church. God knew exactly what He was doing. I respected and loved this woman so much; He knew I wouldn't say no to her.

We started attending her church, and I started drinking less and less. I joined a Bible study and even started singing in the church. I can't remember a time I ever felt as comfortable or loved at a church, but this one sure broke the mold. Everyone was caring and welcoming. I finally found a church home. I had walked through many valleys, but God had never abandoned me. The one who was with me the longest, but who I ignored the most, saw me through every trial.

# Trials and Tribulations

While Stephen was at work and I was home one day, there was a knock on the door. When I opened the door, there were two women standing there. One I recognized from work. I quickly found out she was training to become a CPS worker during the day while working at the call center at night.

"Hello. We are investigating a report that was called in regarding your children. May we come in?"

My heartbeat suddenly became the only thing I could hear.

"Sure. Come in."

We sat down and they laid out their information.

"Someone has called in to report that you have posted online about giving your children Smirnoff."

Confusion was quickly replaced by anger. My mother always called vodka "Smirnoff". I resolved to give them all the information I had from the beginning. My coworker looked right at me.

"I had no idea you were dealing with any of this. At work, you are so happy and always laughing. I am so sorry."

My mask had been perfected over decades. After a week of interviewing my children, they closed the case, and we were in the clear. My mother's words stung me as I recalled them. *You had him charged with a felony and I will have you charged with one too.*

I wish that had been the last of their antics, but it wasn't. Not long after, I received a phone call from a police detective in McKinney. Apparently, Peter had filed a report stating I had stolen money from him in the form of a car payment. I explained the situation. Upon further review, they were able to show where I did not steal any money. I was cleared again. The following week, I was called by another detective stating I was being charged with fraud for writing a check from Peter's business account. When I explained what happened, he requested statements from my husband and me.

When Lea was a few months old, my mother and I had taken her to a doctor's appointment. She continuously struggled with lung problems such as RSV and pneumonia. The appointment required payment. My mother called Peter, and he instructed us to write a check from the business account for the appointment. When I wrote the check, I signed my name. What I didn't understand at the time of writing the check, was that God was protecting me at that moment. My husband was also a partner on the account. Had he not been a partner, permission from him to excuse me from writing the check wouldn't have mattered. He proved to the court that he had permission to use that same business account. Essentially, the Grand Jury decided not to indict me. Another divine accomplishment amid the attacks from the enemy.

After their ploys to destroy us failed, Peter's criminal case was moving along. He finally pled guilty to the charges he was facing. We still had to show up in court to give our testimonies. As hard as it was to face them again, it was the only option for Flora's justice. My newfound love of God coupled with the desire to seek justice for Flora gave me the courage to push forward.

Nobody knew at the time, but my daughter's abuse forced me to finally confront my own sexual abuse. I tried for months to work through the trauma alone but failed. I sought counseling, attended Bible studies, and started going to church. I could not help my daughter without confronting my trauma first. It was the hardest work I have ever had to do because I had to accept what happened and understand that without it, I would not be the person I was becoming. Once I was able to see the purpose for the pain, God made my test a testimony.

I completed the bachelor's degree I started two years prior, followed by a master's degree all the while healing and overcoming battles the devil sent to hinder my faith. Two years after we started attending church, we faced our final battle. Just like an evil boss in a video game, this villain had to be defeated by our testimonies. Our voices were going to be heard.

Peter had summoned my mother, my aunts, my baby sister, and my Nannie to be his character witnesses. The one uncle he didn't call as a witness just happened to be the most gentle, honest, and Christ-like human on this planet. God knew what He was doing. Since my uncle was not a witness, he was allowed to sit and listen to all the testimony. None of them expected our witnesses though. Behind the scenes, Lyn had tracked down Peter's ex-wife and one of his other victims. This victim was raped by him over a decade before he molested my daughter. My mother knew he was on probation with an ankle monitor, but his version of events turned out to be sinister lies. When we found out the truth, we knew just how manipulative and depraved he really was.

Once everyone testified, the prosecutor spoke with us privately. She seemed gleeful.

"Even though he pleaded guilty, I made him tell exactly what he did to your daughter."

I couldn't even speak.

"I was able to compel him to tell the court under oath that your daughter was five years old in May of 2008. During this testimony, he stated he had molested your daughter under her panties and forced her to watch pornographic films. Peter also stated it only happened one time during a sleepover Flora was having with your mother."

My mind began spinning and my heart sank. It never occurred to me that even if my mother was in the house, something like this could happen to her. I forgot one key component when I assessed the risk of him around my children.

"They don't sleep in the same room. I forgot to calculate the possibility of him doing anything to her with my mother's presence. They don't share a room."

The realization reopened wounds inside me I had been trying desperately to heal. The feelings of disappointment, shame, and guilt crept back into the dark spaces of the proverbial lashings I inflicted on myself since we became aware of the abuse. It often felt like the inner work I was doing would never be enough. Even when writing my victim impact statement, I was growing. The unhealed version of myself wanted vengeance. I went from telling him that I hoped he saw the flames of hell behind him every time he looked in the mirror, to telling him that I hoped he felt remorseful at some point and would ask God for forgiveness for his sins.

The gratitude for the prosecutor was unfathomable. In every aspect of these trials and tribulations, God carefully and meticulously worked on my daughter's earthly justice for Peter's sins. Sitting in the courtroom, I glanced around to see his supporters versus my daughter's. He had three rows of supporters. We had four supporters aside from Flora herself. My husband, my older sister, Peter's rape victim, and I sat patiently while waiting for the judge to return from his chambers. Once he was seated, he gave his sentence. Peter John Ellington, the man who came from nowhere and had no living relatives, who thought he found a victim in our daughter, was sentenced to seventy-four years to be served consecutively. At the age of eighty-two, he will be eligible for parole. Justice prevailed; however, the ultimate understanding is that God won the war.

# This is Where the Healing Begins

The sentencing gave us all a huge sigh of relief. After dealing with Peter and my mother for years after we reported him, we finally could breathe. Flora continued counseling, as did I. I also continued seeing my speech therapist, and we often would meet at local trails to walk. She continued to play an integral role in my life. Her guidance, encouragement, and unconditional love healed places within me I didn't even know was possible.

Almost two years after the judge's sentencing, my baby sister contacted me. We had very little contact with each other because she falsely believed Flora lied, and that we had stolen money from our mother and Peter. I missed my relationship with her. To be honest, it had been fractured ever since I graduated from high school. She felt abandoned by me, while I felt she wasn't my responsibility. My feelings were mixed though because I felt an obligation to be responsible for her since Lyn had stepped up to the plate for us all those years ago. Graciously, she stepped up again during these last few years. Lyn continued to be supportive and courageous in times I felt weak.

My baby sister and I met at the local Starbucks and sat outside. Before she could even start speaking, tears rolled down her face.

"I can't tell you how sorry I am. I am so sorry for the pain I have caused you and your family."

I cried too. I absolutely felt betrayed and hurt by her decision to believe them, but I never stopped caring about her. I loved her with all my heart. We had overcome so much.

"Sissy, it's okay. He was a master manipulator and even though she chose him, she was manipulated too. I forgive all of you. Just know that while I forgive, our mother is still not welcome in my life."

She cried even harder and nestled on my shoulder. I didn't care how two snotty-nosed, red-eyed adults looked sitting outside ugly crying. Healing was beginning. God had heard my cries and prayers all those nights I drove home from work drunk.

Every time I crossed over the bridge before home, I prayed I would lose control of the car and drive off the bridge. I truly believed my family was better off without me. I believed that Stephen, Flora, Lea, and Rose would all benefit from my demise. I was so entrenched in pain and desperation that I lost sight of what was most important. Survival. I didn't have to be a victim of my past or circumstances. Neither did Flora. In fact, she was flourishing. She may have had her innocence corrupted by pure evil, but she was an overcomer. A survivor.

My baby sister filled me in on what happened after Peter's sentencing. Apparently, my lone uncle in the court-room audience called my family.

"We got it wrong. He absolutely did this."

Before long, my mother's siblings were calling and mes-saging me. They were apologetic and remorseful for every-thing that had happened. I felt relieved but also sad. Sad at the time we all missed out on. My mother never apologized. She never admitted any wrongdoing. My mother will never be my mom. A mother is someone who gives birth to a child; however, that doesn't mean they love that child uncondition-ally. It also doesn't mean they provide the emotional support they should.

My mother was a runner. She didn't know at the time, and maybe she still doesn't know, but every time something traumatic happened, she ran. She aborted her ultimate mis-sion of being a parent. When she found out my baby sister and I were being molested, she ran. She didn't come back for seven years. When she found out my daughter met the same fate, she bolted. She chose Peter because it was easier. It was easier to stay comfortable over hard work. Healing is hard work. God gave me the most amazing people to help me and my family through these storms. He even brought my speech therapist back to me. My safe harbor.

A mom is someone who gives a child support, encour-agement, and unconditional love freely, whether she gave birth to them or not. I gained a mom who didn't give birth to me. She didn't even raise me. Those two facts don't negate the fact that she has loved me unconditionally and thoroughly supported me throughout my adult life. She didn't give me the gift of life, but God gave me something far better. God gave me the gift of her. My speech therapist patiently mentored me and showered me with God's love to help me endure some of the worst times. When it felt like everything kept crashing down around me, she reminded me of my purpose and God's provisions. My speech therapist was my mom.

In the aftermath of the catastrophes laid before us, Stephen and I decided our family was complete. We were content with our three girls, so I scheduled an appointment to discuss a hysterectomy. Unfortunately, my insurance card didn't arrive in time, so I had to cancel. I was disappointed because my uterus was fighting me from the inside while birth control pills were expanding me on the outside. Such is life.

In 2013, I was still working at the call center. I loved my job. My friends and I were trying to decide on dinner one evening. I requested a local chicken chain I rarely ever requested. I really wanted it though. My friends felt it was weird, but we ate there anyway. Later that night, my friend Simone brought me a pregnancy test.

"You hate Cane's. You must be pregnant. Go take this."

I laughed and thought it was a joke. She didn't. Off I went to the bathroom. There just was no way I was ready for another pregnancy, let alone a fourth child. We were already struggling as it was. My campaign at the call center was on the cusp of closing which meant my commissions checks were about to be obsolete.

*God, I am stressed out, worried, and scared. I can't bring another child into our already depleted household. If I am pregnant, I can't do this without you, God.*

Once I peed on the stick and waited, I continued praying for God's will in my life. I took time to thank God for blessing my life, albeit wrecked like a ship washed ashore. During this silent moment of thanking God, a moment of clarity garnered my attention.

My whole existence had endured storm after storm, tossing me through its crashing waves and damaging me little by little. You can't see my damage on the outside like you can a ship tossed upon the stormy seas; however, my wounds existed. In the midst of all these storms, God sent a lighthouse. A beacon of hope. He sent someone who embodied His love and guidance. Someone who continuously proved to be a safe harbor for that little girl adorned in pink ruffles lying in the fetal position of her office floor all those years ago. The little girl that she carefully and gently picked up and calmed her fears if even for a moment. Here God was, yet again, giving me my safe harbor in the middle of the current storm I found myself in. It didn't matter what that test said. God would provide.

My mom showed me I am worthy of love. She showed God's love through scripture, walks in parks, and meaningful conversations on park benches. God used her to show me just how loveable I am. Her hugs healed small, broken fractures inside me with God's light and love. She is the epitome of a mom, and I am grateful I get to call her mine. After speaking to my husband on the phone, I called my mom.

"I am pregnant."

It turned out my friend was right. I was pregnant with my fourth child. I ended up quitting my job and working from home by starting a home daycare. In June of the following year, I gave birth to our son Matthew. The name Matthew is a male name of Hebrew origin that means "gift of God".

He was the missing piece to our family that we didn't realize we were missing. His life brought so many gifts.

Flora and Matthew instantly bonded. Lea and Rose, although inseparable together, were enamored with him. Rose had been diagnosed with Aspergers along with ADHD. We began noticing changes in her. Matthew was teaching her empathy and love. She struggled in areas concerned with social and emotional development. Their relationship made her blossom. If I had been able to proceed with the hysterectomy, Matthew would not exist. God gave us this precious gift to help our family heal from the trauma and grow in our faith. In retrospect, it is not lost on me that I have gained tenfold what was lost, and I couldn't be more grateful.

# His Mercies are New

Overcoming my sexual trauma while enduring a continuous stream of attacks during my daughter's sexual trauma was not easy. It was raw. It was hard. It was ever-changing. The feelings don't disappear. There isn't some magic potion to make everything whole again. In fact, I could be full of joy one day but crying in despair the next. Through healing, I realized I also had to grieve.

I went through a period of grieving the mother I lost. I had to really work at forgiveness before I could grieve and heal. Forgiving my mother was a process that I had to choose daily. When she crossed my mind, I had to give myself that moment to process the loss and understand that while she didn't fully know the level of depravity her husband possessed, she also didn't have the tools to heal her past. At the same time, I also had to understand that those aren't excuses, rather, reality. Her trauma molded her into who she is today just as mine has. Not everyone overcomes their trauma or heals their inner child. It is the hardest inner work I have ever done and that I will ever do. It was a constant battle in my mind to overcome anger, bitterness, and pity for myself. While grieving the mother I lost, I also had to recognize that I didn't have the mother I deserved either. It was then that I realized I needed to grieve the mother I deserved.

Grieving the mother I deserved was incredibly freeing. I had to sit down and write the qualities of the mother I deserved down so I could properly process and grieve. I mourned for my inner child who never felt worthy of anything but abuse. I also mourned for the nurturing and loving mother I know I deserved. The mother I wish I had. The mother I dreamed she would have been but wasn't. I had to grieve the support, encouragement, active engagement, and unconditional love I didn't get but that I knew I deserved. The mother everyone deserved.

I had to come to terms with the fact that the unhealed version of my mother was her choice because she refused all avenues of professional help to overcome her past. Even when given the option of family with professional help or Peter with no accountability, she still chose to avoid healing and help. The mother I deserved would have chosen her family and professional help to be the best mother and grandmother she could be. Once I went through the grieving process, I felt at peace. I felt like I had thrown the largest boulder of burdens into a bottomless chasm. It was the most overwhelming sense of light pulsating through my body. Though brief, I felt it when I was driving to church one morning.

Once I was done grieving, I was also able to stop the endless mental cycle of unanswerable questions. *Why doesn't she love me? What did I do? How could she say such horrible things about me and my family?* Those are just a fraction of the questions I ruminated on. I was able to release my mother to God's hands full time and continue rebuilding my new life. A life without her. It wasn't easy and it still isn't. It is a daily conversation I must have with God and myself. The woman I now call mom helped me in my walk of faith to help rewire the wrong I had learned throughout my childhood and some of my adulthood. She helped to remind me as often as I needed that this is not my fight alone. That my faith in God was growing and through Him, I could overcome the pain, shame, guilt, and anguish of my upbringing and trauma.

Months after processing my grief and my continuing effort to overcome my trauma, my mom and I would still get together for walks on some of our town's beautiful trails. We can't walk as far anymore due to the aging process, but we are still able to sit on the benches along the path to talk. Our talks are often filled with laughter and scripture. Sometimes, she gives me full truths I didn't know existed. When talking about some of my trauma one day, she revealed the truth about Papa Joe's trial.

"Michelle, I need to tell you something that may upset you."

Anxiety butterflies filled my stomach. While healing helped with so many inner workings, I still struggle with anxiety.

"I'm ready."

She put her arm around my shoulders. I loved her ability to hug or comfort me to ease my anxiety.

"Your mother never reported your abuse. It wasn't you that let him get away."

I was speechless. I had to process this. Over the next few days, I was able to fully accept the fact that my mother would rather blame me, a four-year-old child at the time, for letting a perpetrator get away scot-free than to own up to the fact that she didn't pursue any legal ramifications against this man. I understand my speech delays prohibited my ability to explain what was happening to me at the time, but there was no excuse for my mother not to even try to report him. The only explanation I can remotely understand is that she couldn't face her own trauma and was therefore unable to process and help me through mine. While I understand how hard it is to do that, I will not understand her inability to put my needs before her own. Thankfully, God had already been working in me to forgive her, and I was able to take the information, process it, and move past it. Only God can do that. Once I gave my worries to God over a prolonged period, I was able to get stronger in my faith.

Despite the years of trauma I have endured, I know without God and the people he placed specifically throughout my life and in my path, I would not and could not be where I am or who I am today. Every time I think of myself, I know without a doubt I am a warrior. A warrior, though once wounded, stood tall and brushed the mud, dirt, and clay off. Beneath the layers of hurt, trauma, and muck of life, God rebirthed me brand new. Every hurt, every stumble, every failure, and every ounce of trauma molded me into who I am today. That used to scare me and fill me with self-doubt, but I am no longer a slave to what has happened to me or the scars that I bear. They will continue to be battle wounds that show my story and how God continues to shine His light through my life.

Every day, when I get up in the morning, I know that His mercies are new. Whatever happened yesterday stays there. A new day means new mercies from God and new ways to discover His purpose for me. The fresh start God offers every morning, signifies a constant opportunity to experience His love, forgiveness, and grace. Everyone heals in their own time, and nobody can do it for you. I had to decide I wanted better for my life and start a healing journey that was on God's terms. Not mine.

# There's God's Way or the Hard Way

Healing took many years because I had such an array of trauma to deal with. Sexual trauma contained PTSD, guilt, shame, and trust issues. Growing up with women who were taught not to talk about abuse of any kind and to move on without healing, made me want to heal even more. I did not want to sweep all the dark and terrible atrocities underneath the rug. Once I started my healing journey, those overwhelmingly definitive boundaries became easier and easier to overcome.

Abandonment trauma contained a loss of my sense of self, safety, and stability. When someone left, whether out of town for a few days, or to run an errand away from me, my body would tense up and my anxiety would soar. It felt like I was being left behind every time. When my mom and I reconnected during my healing journey, I learned how to overcome that fear of being left. She travels multiple times a year. Through her travels, I have learned that just because she leaves, nothing changes. She still loves me and always comes back. God knew how to use her in my life to help me overcome the boundaries of fear I relied on for so long.

When Flora was traumatized, it forced me to seek professional help to overcome my own trauma. If I was still suffering, how could I expect to help alleviate my daughter's suffering? The reality was that I had to face my sexual abuse head on. Talking openly about it was hard at first, but eventually, it was freeing. It released shame and guilt from the bondage of sin that it was. It was no longer my burden, but my purpose. I found comfort in being able to talk about the sexual abuse I endured along with the various other types of abuse I experienced along the way because it helped the listener. Many trauma survivors believe they somehow caused what happened to them or that they aren't worth more than what has been done to them. When I was able to start talking to other survivors of trauma, it gave a sense of community when making those connections. Victims just want to be heard, validated, and understood. Once they can make those connections, their victimization changes over to survivor hood.

Finding the right counselor took a bit. I went through three counselors before I found one that I felt the safest with. Honestly, the majority of my hard work was done on the walks with my mom. She, aside from my husband, was the only person I allowed myself to be vulnerable to. In-depth conversations about myself with others were only allowed to go so far before my proverbial wall was erected. I often found myself skipping over some of the more intimate, or dirty details except when she would ask. My mom could ask me anything and I would tell her because I felt like I owed her so much. I could never repay her for the speech work, prayers, walks, discussions, and truths she gave to me over a course of years. God intricately knitted her into my life exactly when I needed her most.

My sisters and I are closer now than we ever have been. While we all three have been on our own healing journeys, we allow ourselves to get together quite often to bond. Growing up, we did not have a close bond between the three of us. With Lyn growing up apart from us, we did not get the chance. I am eternally grateful for the blessing of Lyn's heart of courage because she has been the backbone of our trio. I am equally grateful for the gentle nature of my baby sister and her ability to give grace in any and all circumstances. Including forgiveness for the pain I caused her during our childhood. There is not a day that goes by that I do not regret how my anger and rage affected her.

My mother ended up moving out of state after the demise of her husband. She was so focused on obtaining material things, she missed out on the most important blessing of all. Family. The very things she blamed my daughter for losing, such as her home with the pool and hot tub, ended up being the very things taken from her in the end. She sold off everything she had and fled. She will continue to run from hard things if she does not seek healing from her traumas. It is not lost on me that she has traumas of her own; however, she has the ability to seek professional help. Due to her lack of accountability and her overabundant toxicity, she has yet to be welcomed back in my life. I know she rationalizes her parenting as doing the best she could with what she had at the time; however, there were always chances for her to seek therapy and bipolar treatment, but she refused. She has not met my son. My children do not know her, but they are not lacking. I forgave her for all the abuse, abandonment, and betrayal, but she still isn't allowed in our lives.

Flora graduated high school with honors and is graduating soon from college. She continues to be a well-adjusted woman finding her place in this world. Her story is not my story, but when she is ready to tell it, she will. Her siblings look up to her and know just how courageous she is.

My husband struggles with PTSD from the whole ordeal. He fights inner demons daily due to feeling guilty for what happened. His healing is a work in progress, but he is making huge strides. I am so proud to be his wife. While the man I fell in love with is not the same happy and joyful person he once was, he is continuously trying to heal. His love for our kids and me is always prevalent.

I would not be where I am today without God's faithful provisions in my life. Horrible atrocities have happened to me, but I am able to find purpose regardless. I do not blame God for what happened. Everyone is born with free will. How they choose to use it is up to the individual. The way I see it, I could either wallow in what has happened and focus on things I have lost, or I can live in God's grace and focus on what I have gained.

My dad struggles with his own traumas as well. The one thing nobody can take from him is his overwhelming abundance of love for his children. Through the years, I have learned he loves me for me. If I need him, he comes running. If I needed his shirt, he would take it off and give it to me without question. My memories of him exemplified acts of sacrifice and love. He made sure he was the last person to eat at every meal. If we wanted more, he gave it. I don't know how many nights he went to bed hungry if we ate all the food he made, but it's not lost on me that he did that out of pure love for us. My dad made sure I understood that I was his; therefore, I was a Scott after all.

When my daughter's abuse came to light, we kept it in the light. I know without a doubt I broke a generational curse by doing so. Sexual trauma was evident in at least three generations of us, but there were probably more.

Before my Nannie passed, she invited us to see her. While we missed out on five years of togetherness, we still had three wonderful ones together. My mother never appreciated what she sacrificed to take two children under five and raise them while caring for a dying spouse. At a 90th birthday celebration for her, I reunited with all my aunts, uncles, and cousins. It was such a wonderful reunion. The following year, my Nannie ended up in a nursing home. I visited her as often as I could during her final days.

"Nannie, thank you for all the sacrifices you made raising us. You gave me the best seven years of my life."

Her frail body lay in the bed, still as could be. With her eyes closed, she pointed her face toward the ceiling.

"Best seven years."

She smiled so sweetly. Those would be the last words she ever spoke to me. Once she passed away peacefully, five of her six children handled the after-death process of obituaries, services, and the like. Her funeral was filled with people whose lives she touched. Ella was the only one who didn't attend. After her funeral, I sat on my bed processing my grief and longing for her. As a tear rolled down my cheek, a reminiscent fragrance wafted through the air. It was the scent of Nannie's body powder she used to apply every day. *I love you and miss you too, Nannie.* Only then did I truly believe she was happy and rejoicing in the face of our savior.

God took all my wounds, guilt, shame, and trauma. He then proceeded to fill my life with blessings and purpose. I have enjoyed many years working in childcare, both at home and in a center. When I learn of anyone suffering from trauma, I share my story in hopes it helps them know they can prevail. We have a mighty God who intricately weaves people we need into our lives when we need them in all facets of our lives. He absolutely used the best people in my life every time I needed them. It may appear like nothing phased me or harmed me. Make no mistake. I didn't walk away scot-free from the damage. Nor did I walk away Scott free.